A Mother's Love

A Mother's Love

BASED ON TRUE EVENTS

GABRIELLE GRANT

authorHOUSE®

AuthorHouse™ LLC
1663 Liberty Drive
Bloomington, IN 47403
www.authorhouse.com
Phone: 1-800-839-8640

Published by AuthorHouse 08/29/2014

ISBN: 978-1-4969-3421-5 (sc)
ISBN: 978-1-4969-3422-2 (e)

Any people depicted in stock imagery provided by Thinkstock are models,
and such images are being used for illustrative purposes only.
Certain stock imagery © Thinkstock.

This book is printed on acid-free paper.

Because of the dynamic nature of the Internet, any web addresses or links contained in
this book may have changed since publication and may no longer be valid. The views
expressed in this work are solely those of the author and do not necessarily reflect the
views of the publisher, and the publisher hereby disclaims any responsibility for them.

Dedicated

To
My big sister, Priscilla
I LOVE YOU!!!

CONTENTS

FAMILY INTRODUCTION

OUR MOTHER WAS born into a family of ten, with her being the eldest of them. She was raised by her grandmother and for a short period of time during her teen years she briefly stayed with her mom. Their relationship wasn't the best, but our mom did the best she could to know her mom and she loved her dearly. It was hard for my mom growing up. Her grandmother raised her as I said before, and she was very close to her grandmother. There's many tales of our family history, the struggle. Like most families, they lived a tough life.

Our mother went on to bare seven daughters of her own, my sisters and I. She had never intended to have children of her own. Our mother had the traditional mindset to have a career, be successful, and to be wed. This way if she were to bare any child of her own, she would have support. Unfortunately our mother had been the victim many women still are today and in her youth she did not finish school. When she was older she did home schooling to finish her education.

Poverty swept our mother's lifestyle, and because of the lacking guidance during her teen years, she had lost that sense of direction. After her grandmother died she did not know what was next for her. Her grandmother was all she had. On top of that, she was missing the relationship she should've had with her own mother and no knowledge of who her father was.

This plays a huge role in the story and gives some insight as to why it was so hard for her raising her own daughters. With no father active in our lives, we had to endure our childhood with an empty void that remains still today. Like many women, we long and search to fulfill this void. Our mother too searched in all the wrong possible places to fill every empty void she had in her life, in her heart.

She is a great woman and a wonderful mother. She raised us to forgive and to always keep prayer in our lives and to stay strong in the word of God. We grew up in church and said our prayers every night. She sent us all on our way with the bible. Her grandmother had done the same for her.

In spite of her faults and mistakes, we've never stopped loving her and never will. She is our mother, though many times we disagree with her choices. She raised us to fear her and to be obedient. At times we failed at that and would have to reap the disciplinary consequences she had in store for us.

We'll never be able to fathom why she did a lot of the things she did. God had mercy on her anyway. We all suffer some guilt and even denial.

PROLOGUE: (GOOD TIMES)

"Come and sit with me" she'd say.
And let's watch TV all day
I'd smile and sit with her watching TV
While we waited for dinner so we could eat

"I like this show, hope it comes on again
Let's watch a movie, I like movies
You like movies Gab?"
Yes I like movies, what do you want to see?
And we'd stay up and watch movies til she fell asleep

Good times they were
We shared as many of them as we could
It was the simple things that mattered to her
Like talking, laughing, and watching TV
Then eating good food, saying goodnight to mom and me

When we'd walk and go to the park
Or play the only card game she could play
Match
Or we'd go in the front yard and play catch

She liked reading stories as a child, even as an adult
She loved music with a passion
Knew every song on the radio
She liked drawing and putting puzzles together
We'd sit and do them whenever she wanted
Unless I just didn't feel like it
Then she'd do her own puzzle and then show me
I'd tell her good job and then do one with her
When mom wasn't home we'd blast the radio
Then dance together til we were beat tired
Some times mother would come home to us asleep on the couch
Or even the floor
Good Times

BEGINNING

I AM BUT a new born. Even that not quite and still yet my dear mother pretty much hates the thought of me in her life. The existence of my twin and I, brings disgust to my mother but still I try to be her friend.

Mind you I am still not yet born. I am but a new born. She will bare me until the womb can take no more. She will give birth to me and one more. I love her I do, if she only knew. She doesn't understand the love that I possess. It is plain and clear even the blind could see, a child who so deeply loves her mother.

She will bare me 6 months longer. She will feel my sister and I grow. With each day that passes by she realizes her answer is no. She wishes harm upon me, she does not want my growth. She hates me already and my face I've not yet shown. I am afraid to be born and I want a mother's love. I am afraid the woman scorned won't give herself a chance to love.

To be a mom and nurture me, sing me songs while rocking me to sleep. No yelling or shouting for things I don't know. No beatings for things I do not know. I learn slower than most people do. I don't know better, my spirit forever young. Only if my mother loved me, there would be no harm done.

Still a new born and I am almost ready to come out. Little does my mother know, upon me a mental illness has fallen. I will be sick and may God's mercy reign. My mother is wicked and angry with pain. She will inflict me and strike me over and over. Pain no child should have to suffer.

I am born and my sister too. My mother couldn't handle the truth. One twin is fine, the other not so much. My twin had taken most of the nutrition unfortunately so I had been given medication.

Apparently it was the wrong injection because by the end of it, the discovery was a mental illness. My head was shaved bald and needle marks covered the back of my head. My stomach had been cut open from my inability to digest.

For what reason do you hate me? Why don't you like me? I will fight hard for your love inspite of it. Oh mother! Oh mother why! Why must every tear I cry be of the pain you've caused me, WHY?!

Still a baby I am, and in doctors care for about a month or two. And I notice there's a Nurse named Gwen. She loves me as a mother should. She never judged me and I don't think she could. She took care of me, and gave me kindness and protection. The sad fact of it all was that it would only be temporary, and there may have been some guilt behind it. She had known all along about the wrong injection I had been given. So she pretty much did everything she could for my mom and me.

All my life there's been no heaven. To hell and back with my mother I go, longing the return of Nurse Gwen until next time. Nurse Gwen would send me gifts. I was sick and needed treatment and medication. Nurse Gwen cared for me; she did everything that my mother did not. About 3 months I had become, with swollen eyes, my conscious gone. My mother had struck me once or twice, and all I can remember is the devil in her eyes.

I had not yet begun to talk. A mental illness took over my world. I was slow, but no less the human my mother is. My other sisters would mourn for me, I wasn't the only kid. I thought maybe one day it would all be fine. Thought the pain would go away in due time.

But my mother stayed the same; let me cry aloud for hours. Gag food down my throat, just so I'd holler even louder. She was evil full of hatred. And so I screamed for sweet Nurse Gwen. Begging to God she'd come see me, visit me again, save me from death. Take me away, for this woman I have no breathe left. No life left. She has stripped away my smile.

I lay awake each night; my voice is gone and all cried away. Morning is here, the sun has come up and the witch is back and out to play. Nurse Gwen! Nurse Gwen! You've finally come!! Nurse

Gwen! Nurse Gwen! Please take me from here and don't ever look back. This place is a wreck and my mother does not love me. Deeper and deeper into sorrow I drown, I hurt every night. See this sore on my lip, mother thought that was alright. Mother keeps hitting me and my sisters can't help. Poor sisters they mourn for me, she's scared them to death.

Come Nurse Gwen, let's be on our way. I'm a year old now and can't walk or talk today. I tried walking but mother called me dumb. I tried talking but mother says I'm dumb.

And my twin yes she sees this, but what can she do. My twin yes she is also a year old too. Nurse Gwen would come over every now and then, but not often enough. I hated when she left because I knew what would come next. Sometimes she would take me to her house. It felt like God had given me a break. It was only a matter of time before I'd end up back with the witch.

Nurse Gwen please don't take me back. I cannot take anymore of this. My eye will be swollen again and my back too covered in sores. You'd think she hated both my twin and I but clearly I was all alone. The only one she excessively beat. She may not have been as fond of everyone else but she only hated me. What had I done but be born innocent. And every child loves their mother. For me, my mother had no love in her. She was bitter and I had only just turned two.

It was difficult for me to talk, and even more difficult for me to walk. I wish she had more patience and more care in her heart. For me she gave no damn, cause her heart was rotten. So my sisters had taught me to take steps. And my mother, believe me she didn't like it one bit. They would teach me a lot.

How to eat, hold my spoon, and even to use the bathroom. If it was up to mother, she would shout at me. Tell me I'm stupid and then tell me to just get up and get out. She'd tell me I can't learn anything. Called me dumb like my dad, and for him I'm sure her heart grew cold. He must have caused her great pain for her to hate me so much and treat me this way.

I want my mother. I missed her when she'd leave. Whenever she'd return I'd jump up because I was happy. Quickly she would tell me to go sit down somewhere. The sweetest embrace, it drove me insane. I longed to hug her, to know what a mother's big hug felt like. I was only three and couldn't even hurt a bug. I am gentle and kind even when I'm doped up on meds, which was all the time. Because I had a bit of a mental illness, I didn't deserve a good life. But I loved her so even though she despised me. I wasn't allowed to look and feel pretty. It was almost impossible any how with so many beatings.

Yes! Nurse Gwen! Back to rescue me! She had come back. I called Nurse Gwen my friend. The look on her face, she was sad and afraid for me. She had realized where all those scars had come from. But there was nothing she felt she could do. Mother must have threatened Nurse Gwen.

I may not have survived so long had it not been for sweet Nurse Gwen. I'll be four years old soon. And this morning I woke up with a knot on the back of my head. I forgot it was there. My mom was mad at me again. And yet I am only going to be four years old soon. Because of my disability, am I not a human? I too have feelings and they hurt so badly. For my mother I am desperate to feel warmth and security.

Will she ever love me? What can I do to make her feel better? How can I make her smile? I tried drawing her a picture once and she told me I cannot draw and that it was an ugly picture just like me. So I drew Nurse Gwen a picture and she put it up on her fridge. It made me smile because she reminded me that people can be kind. Politeness did exist and Nurse Gwen loved me. But mother did not. And I am helpless, I cannot do anything. Maybe if I was different she would've loved me.

For me and my twin's birthday Nurse Gwen made us a cake. It was so good. Mother made hot dogs and chili and gave us all candy and soda. Nurse Gwen helped me blow out my candles. Soon the party ended, all my sisters began to clean up and soon it would be time for bed I couldn't sleep much at night. My mother would come and wake me up to make sure I had not wet the bed. She would beat me if I did and if not then she'd make me go pee and yell at me. A woman so cruel and unfair, I loved her though. Unconditionally, the way she should've always loved me.

My sisters would rush home everyday from school. They never knew if I was alright or not. Some would question why my mother had not been reported. Fear of being separated seemed to be the issue. We were all very close.

Most days mother would tape up my black eye. Send me off to school just that way. My clothes she cared not to make them decent. And oh lord my hair. When she did do it, it was the worse times of my life. If she were using the hot comb, my scalp would be raw in some areas. She would pull and tug away at my hair for no good reason. Again I was helpless and I had to endure. But why me?

The sores in my scalp no barrette could hide. Raw wounds against my ear where the hot comb had been. She would inflict as much pain upon me as she could. And I could not cry. She would tell me not to. Of course I did, but that meant more pain to come.

Mother leaves for work and I run after her for a hug. Just the way I always do. And the usual is what I'd get in return. She will ignore me and look away. Or even better, just tell me to go sit down somewhere and watch TV or go play with my doll babies. She didn't want any of my sisters to tolerate me at all. They were supposed to learn from the pain that she caused.

They had seen mother put me down so much they didn't know what to comprehend. They wondered themselves sometimes, why is it that mom is always frustrated with our little sister? What can we do to help? But the truth was that they would suffer verbal abuse for trying to defend me. They were always afraid for me. I was a little fragile light weight. Thin to the bone and weak from being struck. My only strength was to keep loving her and to survive.

All I could do was hope. By this time I was six years old. It's a good thing I was drugged up on medication just about my whole life. It took away all the bad memories. But I can never forget the one thing missing from my soul, my heart, a mother's love. That's all the healing I needed to recover. Just to know that she loved me. I had already forgiven her.

My heart ached everyday to put the pieces together. I loved puzzles. Nurse Gwen taught me to put puzzles together. Every time I spent at her house I played with her cat and her daughter. They would put puzzles together with me sometimes.

But then I started to get angry. Emotions unknown began to unleash and overwhelm me. I began acting out from time to time. School caught it too. The storm had not past and there was still more bad weather to come.

The teachers would call home. Yes I was afraid, but I knew what to expect. Before I could even make it inside, there was a blow straight to my head, then again to my mouth for crying out. She had beat me into a seize. I had seized up and began to shiver and my breathing became uneasy. There were lashes everywhere all across my body. I bled and bled and when I could breathe normal again, the tears had not yet ended.

Already I've lived a tough enough life. You'd think I had enough, but there's always more in store. Mother was never done. The horror was ongoing until the end of time because I was never going to get her love.

MIDDLE

I AM BUT a child. Yesterday was my eighth birthday. My sister's are away at school and today I get out of school early. Today I told the teacher "no" and to "shut up". I was upset and couldn't control my anger. This was on and off at times. There were days at home when I would get upset and get in trouble for expressing emotion.

Sure enough that day I came home to a complete episode. Mother was always enthusiastic about whoopin' my ass. She beat me with an extension cord, all of us really. Then to top it off she'd even use her foot sometimes. Threw me around and ripped my shirt up. Again I ask myself why me? Yes I am a bit mentally challenged, but that is not my fault. I am an outcast to my family. My mother has proved that to be true.

She loves to embarrass me and laugh at me. She fed off her hatred toward me. Later that night I had taken a bath and she came in to rush me out. Then a little water splashed onto the bathroom floor. Crazy she went and terror filled my heart. Her temper with me affected my own temper. She dragged me out of the tub, forcing me to clean up the water. A very small amount then became even more from the water dripping off of my body.

I cleaned it up the best I could, but of course I myself aren't enough. She belittled my capabilities. Mother had come back to check and was not satisfied. She would always make a reason to beat me up. Box me down and slap me around.

With my baby sister on the way, that might have given me a break. Nurse Gwen will come today and see the scars I wear all over. Just the other day, I had gone to school exactly the way I appear now. Mother did not care. Finally Nurse Gwen had arrived. I had my bags packed and ready to go.

Excited for my stay with Gwen I ran to the car. Mother, I'm sure was very glad to be rid of me. Every time before I'd step out the door I would turn to her and say "bye ma! I love you! I'm gonna miss you mama!" Inside my soul was sad that she never missed me.

Holidays coming soon and I'm full of cheer. That's a bad thing in mother's eyes. I loved thanksgiving because of all the good food. From being threatened and forced to eat so much I finished my food before everyone sometimes. This time I threw some of it up and mother decided she didn't like that. So she forced me to eat the remains I had thrown up. I gagged and she hit me.

My older sisters washed the dishes and cleaned up everything. After my beating I went to bed. Mother woke me to take a bath. My body still raw, I get into the tub and immediately flinch to the touch of water. She made sure to add bubbles just for me. I was in pain and angry. Sometimes I felt that if that was the only attention I would get from her then so be it. I got so frustrated most times I would purposely misbehave just for her.

Mother was 7 months and Christmas was just around the corner. I didn't understand where babies came from. I just knew I was getting a baby sister. Will mother beat her too? Maybe I'm just an alien to her. Slowly mother manipulates us all. I began to believe that I couldn't read because she called me so many things like dumb, stupid, ignorant, stupid ass, dumb ass, and even retard. Who gets lucky enough to have their very own bully at home?

Christmas is here and Ms. Gwen comes by. She brought gifts for everyone. She was certainly my guardian angel. I couldn't wait to open my gifts, and to see what my sisters got. They were excited, we all were and no one could wait to eat Christmas dinner.

Mothers' ultimate goal was always to ruin every fun experience for me. Mother was convinced that it was the fault of Nurse Gwen and the hospital for my minor mental illness. She thought of suing. But who knows the cause. She doesn't even know what's wrong with me. I doubt she even knows what it is called.

The night was over and snow had fallen. It was beautiful and I was excited. This is probably the one time I got to enjoy something without mother ruining it. She let me and my older sisters go out and play in the snow. I didn't even try to figure out why suddenly everything felt ok. It would not last, but I enjoyed the moment anyway.

Baby Hope had been born and though I didn't understand everything, her smile made me happy. Mother even let me hold her. Mother completely disregarded any possibility of me learning. She asked me one day to name all my sisters. She had not taught me anything, but my sisters did. I named them all in order from oldest down to baby Hope. I pointed at each of them, Elaine, Olivia, Peyton, Allison, my twin Penelope, me Gracie and the new baby Hope. Mother was confused and could not believe it.

She was even a little upset about it and wanted to know who taught me. I told her they each taught me there names. She could not believe it. A doubt so strong even the truth left her speechless. What was I to do? They couldn't convince her either. This made me feel bad. My own mother has no faith in me.

Mother is home now and the new baby is sweet and happy. She looks at me and smiles. She doesn't even know me and for now she loves me just as I am. My dear baby sister is so cute and I can't wait to play with her. She cries sometimes then mother gives her a bottle and she stops.

I tried playing with Hope but Mother wouldn't let me. She's only one year old now and my sisters get to play with her. It's not fair but then again that's the way it's always been for me. I felt alone at home and I was alone at school too. Mother said no one was my friend and that nobody wanted to be and I'd try to tell her that I had friends at school and she would insult and make fun of me.

Nurse Gwen is old, very old. She takes good care of herself and her husband. She would always bring clothes and coats, shoes and school stuff for me and my twin sister. She'd help my mom out with groceries and pretty much anything she needed. Mrs. Gwen just didn't know mother had given most of my clothes to my other sisters if they could wear them, once again unfair.

Everyday I'd look in the mirror and just stare. I'd stand there hoping my life would change. Wondering why things had to be this way. Would she always be angry, always stay mad? Would I always be the blame and left all alone to be sad? No one deserves to be treated like this. She hates my guts and she's filled with disgust.

Baby Hope is now 3 years old and very playful. Nurse Gwen loves Hope. We all do. Hope plays with me and enjoys me. Of course mothers' next target was Hope. She intended to manipulate my baby sister into disliking me. And for what? Because she couldn't tolerate me? I honestly don't think mother ever accepted that she would be giving birth to twins whether she wanted us or not. She could have aborted us. That would've spared us all the pain and misery caused.

Nobody should hate life. Let alone have the gift to bring into the world another life, only to abuse and manipulate and mistreat them. I may as well had been burning in hell all this time.

My baby sister and I grew closer and closer. But nothing kept mother from preventing any kind of bond between us. I wasn't even close to my own twin. Mother placed tension between us, negative tension.

She intentionally treated her better than me and she made sure I saw it. She wanted me to see her love my twin and give my twin the attention I was so desperate for. Sometimes my sister and I would play together. They all thought that because I was a bit mentally challenged, that I couldn't tell the difference between love and hate.

I could tell the difference most definitely. They were fools if they thought otherwise. Things are the same, they haven't changed nor will they ever change. My soul still filled with sorrow and more sorrow. Drowning in the pain of emptiness and on with the search for a mother's love. Not Mrs. Gwen.

Hope is almost four. She is my sister. There are times when my memory fades and all I remember is that my sisters are family. I don't know why I forget, but the medication plays a role in it. I take two different things for depression and my temper. Mother lies about my scars, and tells the doctors I need more meds. This is why I'm so forgetful. So sometimes I just say things out loud like "you are my sister". It helps me reassure myself that they are not strangers.

I'm up and ready for school and excited to see my friends and to tell my sisters about my new friends. It was proof that mother is a liar. I can have friends and they like me. They play with me, learn with me, and talk to me. I have a boyfriend too. Mother doesn't like it when I talk about them though.

"Hurry up! Eat all of your food and clean that whole plate when you're done! Miss the bus and I'm gonna beat your ass!" This is mom pretty much every morning. She'll scream at me to wake me up each morning for school. Bang against the walls and beat on the door just to scare me to death... Every single morning. And I ask myself til this day, "how did I survive?"

I had not yet finished my breakfast and I had already braced myself for a blow to my face. She hit me with all her might. One hit took me out of my chair. The bus was outside already and I was getting beat up. She threw food at me and threw my jacket at me. Then shoved me out the door with my book bag and I walked up to the bus in tears.

Just how much longer was I to endure this agony?? She hates me! I get it. So just make this easy for us all and simply put me out of my misery. I'm tired, and alone. I need help. The cry for help screams inside me and people see but they don't understand.

I finally arrive at school and I was ready to see my friends and classmates. I'm always excited to play and learn. I sat next to the boy I liked but then my temper got in the way. "Don't sit by me. Leave me alone, don't talk to me. I don't like you, go away!" I said this to him, and my teacher heard me saying this and made me sit up front. I spit at the boy and then my teacher threatened to call my mom. I quickly took my seat then put my head down to cry. My teacher thought that I was crying because she was going to tell on me. I was really crying because I was already going to be beaten anyway. Instead of her trying to be there for me, she only took the time to be my teacher and nothing more.

It was lunch time so we lined up and headed to lunch. I got in line behind the boy I liked and told him I was sorry and that I still like him. He hugged me and said ok. So I guess that was it.

Home sweet home. I washed up to get a snack and went outside with my sister to play. Mom came outside and said Mrs. Gwen was coming over for dinner. Seconds later I turn around and she was pulling into the drive way. My heart was warm whenever she was around. I felt safe and free. We helped her with bags of groceries and then we went back outside to play. I couldn't resist grabbing another snack, so I did. Mother took it from me and told me to wait and to get out of the kitchen.

Dinner was finally ready and we were all hungry. We got washed up for dinner and it was great. Pot roast with potatoes, green beans and rice. Then we had some blueberry muffins after that. I was full and Mrs. Gwen had to go. Of course I never wanted her to leave my side. I gave her a really big hug and then I was rushed off to bed.

Morning came too soon. I woke up to that woman banging on my walls and slamming the door open again. Some days I'd already be up waiting for her to come in wild to wake me. I could wash up, brush my teeth and be dressed in time for breakfast. Then mother would have one less reason to torture me.

So I'm done with breakfast and out the door. I say to mother "see you later, love you ma!" then the door slams so I stop waving and I get on the bus. As the bus drives away I look back and stare out the window at my house. Hoping she'd at least wave back. But all the windows were covered by our curtains.

"Hey Penelop, you like school?", I had tried to say her name right, but it got better over time. "Yeah it was fun. You like school Gracie?" "Yeah I have three friends. You want to know their names?" "What are their names?"

I loved talking about school and my friends. I would ask all of my sisters about school. I'd even ask them if they had boyfriends. Mother didn't like that either. So I eventually stopped asking. But it wasn't long before I was back at it again. It wasn't fair to me, they had boyfriends and talked about them but I wasn't allowed to even think about any of that. I go through puberty and every phase any girl goes through. Did I not deserve to have those wants and needs?

CLIMAX

I AM BUT a teen, barely yet. My mother is still the same. I have to remember I have six sisters and I have to remember their names. Elaine, Olivia, Peyton, Allison, and my twin Penelope and baby Hope. She's getting big now. I am fourteen and baby hope is six. My older sisters are out of the house now and on their own. It is only me, my twin, and Allison she's fifteen. And we are also aunts.

Thanksgiving is coming up and I can't wait! My big sisters will be here and we'll all gather around to say what we're thankful for. They always make everyone go around and say what they're thankful for. We record it and the big ones go first then the little ones. I loved saying what I was thankful for. I said the same thing every time. "I'm thankful for my family, mom, my school, my teacher, my friends, food and God." Everyone would clap and cheer then the next person went.

Family time was the best. No fighting, no arguing and plenty food. Laughing and talking was all there was. But it never lasts. There would always be those times when a dramatic scene would happen. No serious damage would be done. But it was enough to scare the children. And then of course like most families, we'd reunite as if nothing ever happened. I love my sisters very much.

Christmas is near, and its time for winter break. One thing I always looked forward to was Mrs. Gwen bringing gifts. She'd bring something for everyone. Though most of them were for Penelope and I. Of course mother only gave me what she wanted me to have. The rest would be distributed to Allison if she could fit it, and to Penelope. Had I understood this was going on I would've taken them back.

Winter break is here so no school. I hadn't seen it snow much at all here in South Carolina, but it finally came down. Mother let us go outside and play in it. When the sun had set it was time to come in, wash up and eat. Mother had decided she didn't like the way my room had looked. Toys were out that my sister and I had. My bed wasn't made from the nap I took after school. So we ate our dinner, then we took our baths.

Mother caught me fresh out of the tub. Swift strikes with the extension cord sliced my body left and right. She caught my face and got me across my chest. By the end of it, I had been covered and there was blood.

I had to clean up what little mess there was in our room. My sister was not touched. We had got into bed after and fallen asleep.

Hours passed and mothers routine was on its way. Every night, in the middle of the night, she'd bust open the door to my room then bang on the walls. She was a bully to me for what reason? Who knows.

Her goal was to terrify me and at that she succeeded every time. I'd wake up shaking, trembles everywhere, then she'd shout "GET UP!! Go pee and hurry up!" God forbid I wasn't up and moving. She'd grab the nearest object to her and launch it right at me. I swear she was unconscious whenever she'd beat me because the poor woman could never stop.

I was lucky to try to make it to the bathroom before she got to my room. I hated it when she would do that. That lady hated her own child. Most people do though. I'll never understand it. But I'll love her to the end of time. It pains me deeply that I can't get through to her. I wish there was something my sisters could do, Mrs. Gwen or somebody. Mrs. Gwen has to be careful when she reaches out to me. Mother likes to give warning with the threat of never seeing me again.

I don't believe I would've lasted so long had God not sent Mrs. Gwen to be my Guardian Angel.

Mom is putting me in camp. I'm excited, but she just wants to see less of me. That hurts, but I smile anyway. I'd bring back pictures I'd drawn for her. She threw them all away. I would draw the best pink hearts I could and even tried drawing people in a house. Those people were her, my sisters and I.

Why couldn't she see that I was still normal? I'm alright. My mental disability isn't my fault. I think of her, and I want so badly for her to just hold me tight in her arms and tell me she loves me. I try to behave just for her and in return she'll do her best to ignore me. What could I do to get through to her rotted heart?

I tried telling her about the fun I had at camp and the friends I made. She'd say "What did you learn at camp! You probably don't remember. Never mind go put your bag away." I tried telling her we learned about mixing colors and painting. I even brought a painting for her but she wouldn't give me a chance to show her. My sisters had asked to see it.

They'd get excited and say I did a good job. But I wanted to show mom. And she didn't care to see it. So I showed them then sat it on my dresser. I got washed up for dinner, and then we all went to bed. Every night before bed we'd say our prayers and then say goodnight to each other. Of course she wouldn't even say that to me.

The weekend is finally here. Hope and I are playing with our toys together. Lunch time came around so fast. We ate and then went outside to play. Sunset had come too soon, and then the moon met the sky. We had to go inside and get ready to eat again. Dinner smelt great and I was hungry. Finished my food then off to bed and we do it all over again tomorrow.

Church in the morning and we had to put on our ugly dresses. I only understood that in church we needed to be quiet. I was just supposed to understand that God is good and he is my friend. So that's what I believed until the next Sunday. My memory would flush and the only refresher was prayer before we went to sleep and church every Sunday.

It's a normal day like any other. Home from school and my homework is to write my name, home number, and address. I did very well. Spelled my name right and wrote our home number and asked one of my sisters for our address. Mother seemed pleased, but I could tell her hopes weren't up at all.

8th grade graduation coming up and my twin and I are excited. We each had our white dresses for graduation. Mrs. Gwen was so proud and little Hope was just happy. My older sisters helped get us ready for the ceremony. Our special day is tomorrow.

We're up early to make sure we're all ready and early to our ceremony. We look very pretty, and we've eaten breakfast already. Finally we get there and get to our assigned seats. I just followed my teacher to where my class was sitting. The ceremony began shortly after we were seated. Soon my class had to stand, and then make a line. We were in order by alphabet.

They called my name and my family broke the rules. They jumped up screaming and cheering for me and my sisters Penelope and Allison. My two nephews were so little. Cameras were snapping everywhere and I just looked around with a huge smile on my face.

Home sweet home! Family all around and food to be eaten. So that's what we did. We ate, and ate, then relaxed and watched television. My older sisters left, and then it was time to go to bed. We got washed up, then went to bed.

Here she comes in the middle of the night again. I can hear her stomp the yard down the hall to my room. She'd wake my sisters up too. Boom! There she goes banging on the walls. She was determined to express every bit of hatred she felt toward me. {Now I realize the sorrow Precious felt in her heart} I quickly slip into my bedroom shoes and run into the bathroom pissing out of fear. Finally I'm done and she leaves me alone.

I wake up to mother burning grits. The alarms in the house woke us all up. She yelled at us to get freshened up. So we did and we hurried. Got back in time for breakfast, then outside to play.

Later tonight she's going to braid my hair up. It's always horrifying when she does my hair. She'll ring my neck and bend my head in several uncomfortable positions. She'd beat my head if she saw me try to move to get comfortable. She'd pull my hair til she knew there would be a sore to come later. My scalp would usually be raw and stained here and there with blood.

There would be scratches on my neck from her beating me with the comb. Pain grew heavy on my heart year after year, month after month, day by day, every hour every minute. When would this all end? Cutting my wrist won't do the trick. So may there be some hope? Maybe there will be a light at the end of the tunnel for me....

Sure enough I woke up with sores in my head and for my head ache she would not give me any medicine.

CLOSING

I AM STILL young and becoming. It's high school for me now. I can't forget I have sisters and more nieces and nephews now. I enjoy going to school and learning with my friends. Hope is in elementary still.

Sometimes she'd help me with my letters and we'd do math. She tried helping me remember and it worked for a little while. After getting told all your life that you're dumb and stupid, you don't remember anything. You sort of get the mindset that you can't learn anything. So my temper began to shorten and I'd tell Hope I didn't want to learn anymore. She didn't understand, but I was discouraged mentally and emotionally. Mother had guaranteed I wasn't capable and so this led me to believe no one should waste their time teaching me.

Even in school at times I'd get short tempered for no reason. I couldn't control it. I was angry and the medication didn't stop me. I don't think anything would. Eventually mother went up on my medication so I'd just go to bed earlier than normal.

Home from school, it's the weekend and I have no homework. It would've been a good day except my sisters decided they weren't getting along again. They fought every now and then. I don't know why, but they didn't really like each other much. I even asked Hope one day why didn't they like each other and she said she didn't know either.

They both ended up getting whooped for fighting. I never like seeing my sisters get in trouble. I'd always hug them and ask if they were ok. Even with Hope.

I asked mother could I go back to camp again for the summer and she said no. My behavior was out of control sometimes so they couldn't tolerate me. But they'd never guess why I acted out so much. I told mom I was sorry and that I wouldn't do it again. She told me to shut up and watch TV. I said no to her and argued her to let me go back. She'd threaten to beat me if I decided to keep going.

Came home from school the next day and saw a guy up the street. I decided to try and talk to him since mother said boys don't like me and that I couldn't make them talk to me.

I went up the street and kept on walking. Someone brought me back home and told my mom I was wondering the street. I told her I was following a man and she told me he doesn't want me. She said he probably thought I was crazy because I followed him.

I told her no. I started shouting at her. She told me to sit down before she hurt me. I guess the older I got, the less afraid I was of her. She could only do as much harm to me as she has already done my whole life.

Another family gathering it is! My nieces and nephews are here to visit. I see them every now and then. I've missed them and I'm excited every time they come over. I chase them around and we play hide and seek.

Food is almost ready and we all gather around to get ready to eat. The older ones ate in the living room and the children and I ate in the dining area. Once we finished, I had to take my medicine then go on to bed. So I did. Then everyone came into the room and watched TV while I was trying to sleep. My little niece began jumping up and down on top of my bed.

I had told her to get down but she was stubborn. Though she was a child and did not understand my knee was still fragile with no support, she ended up jumping on it. We all know what's next. My knee began to shift out of place and I was in pain all over again.

The ambulance came fast and strapped me up like last time. My sisters were in tears and I was in pain. They felt guilty for not properly supervising her. Had they, this could have been avoided.

I've endured too much pain in my life time. The blessing in disguise is that most don't live through it. But me, I did. Still here and can't remember any of this. The rest of my sister's wait up for my return. I made it home safe with mom and back in a brace.

I wore the brace for a few weeks. Mother helped me out a little bit more this time. I was shocked. Couldn't believe how her attitude took a slight shift. Of course it didn't last. Never did, never would and never will. Still I love her dearly. She is my mother and I am her daughter. She hasn't yet accepted me into her heart or her life. But I'll always want her in mine.

Up goes the dosage in my medication. She lied to the psychiatrist that would see me every now and then. She thought for some reason that they wouldn't see the scars she put on me, or the scratches. But they did.

And here's what she'd say, "She hurts herself. She scratches herself sometimes. Sometimes she acts crazy." So they consulted on depression medication, something that would have a stronger affect on my moods. Like that affected any decision I made. Drowsiness was the biggest affect any of the medication had on me period.

Everything else was mostly from natural causes. She provoked anger in me. I didn't like taking the medication. It was always nasty.

We're moving today and it's also me and my sister's last year of high school. I don't want to stop going to school. Mother is going to put me in a program with other young adults and teens that have finished high school. It's called some kind of workshop. We do activities and fun stuff. They take us on field trips and everything.

Mrs. Gwen comes around less. She's getting old so I understand I guess. Mom says Mrs. Gwen is getting old and for me not to expect her to come around all the time. I didn't like it but I couldn't change it. She still did things for us.

She always helped with groceries and household items we might need. I missed her a lot. Mom really hurt my feelings one day. She was doing my hair and well you know, up to her same ways. Pulling and tugging at my hair. I struggled to ask her when I could see Mrs. Gwen again.

She told me Mrs. Gwen didn't want to see me again. She said that Mrs. Gwen didn't want to be around me because I didn't know how to act. I began to cry uncontrollably. That was a first. I usually cried because of her beating. This time, she definitely hurt my feelings.

And it gets better. She made me feel like I had a disease every time I tried to hug her or show any type of affection toward her. She called me gay a few times and told Hope (who was now in middle school) that she thinks I like girls. When I over heard this I was bothered by it very much. I told her no, and that I like boys.

One day I was convinced I was gay. Made me go a little crazy, and I cut all my hair off.

It was her fault, once again. Hope had come back from school that day in jaw dropping awe. She couldn't believe what I had done. There I stood at the top of the stairwell looking down at her. I told her not to tell mother. Failing to realize mom would simply see it. I was bald.

I told Hope that I was a boy, that I liked girls. I told her I thought girls were cute. She told me to stay in my room until mom came home. She didn't know what to say or do. Eventually I came on downstairs anyway. Sat and talked to her until mom came home. Hope told me I wasn't gay and that I like boys and boys like me. She tried to make things better. But it was too late and all my hair had covered my dresser.

Mother is unlocking the door and Hope and I are bracing for moms shocking response. The door opens and she looks at me, and then turns to shut the door. She turns back and says "Oh my God!! What did she do to her hair! All her pretty hair!" like she really gave a damn. She told me to go upstairs and stay in my room.

Eventually enough time had gone by, and my hair had grown back. By then, I was after men again. Oh and we moved again for the thousandth time. Hope was starting high school now. I had been put into a different workshop.

I couldn't wait to get out of the house to go there. Made a few friends and went on more field trips. It was fun and took my mind off my mom for awhile. Not all the time, but for the most part it did.

Mom and I got into it again. About how no one wants to be my friend. We ended up fighting. Of course she beat me up and I couldn't stop her. When my sister had got home from school my eye was bruised and my lip had been split. Mom had left the house to see a friend up the street. Hope was furious and asked me if I was alright. She asked me what happened. I told her mom fought me. I told her mom beat me up and punched me in the face.

Hope waited up for mother to get home. I had gone to bed, but not quite fallen asleep yet. I heard mom come in. Hope didn't speak to her at all. I'm sure mom could tell she was upset. Mom asked her had she seen my face. Hope answered yes.

Then mom goes on to say she had to defend herself to me because I'm crazy. She told Hope that I'm strong and she had to fight me for real for me to calm down.

Now in most cases this could be true. Some mentally disabled adults are very strong and need to be restrained. Not beat up. As I said before, she was up to her normal nonsense again. Hope didn't fall for her lie and went off to bed.

Mother should feel bad. She lied a lot. It was a sad shame but she stuck with her bullshit stories. One of these days she'd realize how ignorant it was of her to do these things.

The facility called and asked about my lip. It had clearly still been freshly busted open. She proceeded to lie to them as well.

Of course they didn't buy it either. They told her if they saw another bruise anywhere on me they'd report her. Soon she took me out of that program to cover her own ass.

START OF THE END

⁂

I AM AN adult and still young... mother has decided that it's been awhile, and its time to put me in another program. I'm excited I guess. I'd like to spend some time with her. Of course she doesn't really ever want or intend to spend time with me. Every time I think about it, the program just might be a better alternative.

It's been a couple days now and she's finally heard from the facility. They say I can start first thing Monday. I'm hyped about that and I ran to Hope and told her before mom could. Hope was happy for me. She gave me a big hug and I told her I love her. She always said it back and it made me smile.

Mother never liked it, but didn't say anything whenever it happened. Hope is my baby sister and I am her big sister. Hope went to mom and asked to know more about the program and what I'd be doing. I eventually interrupted them to say I'm going to make new friends and get myself another boyfriend.

Here we go again. Mother and I argue again, and then she tells me if I keep going she'll send me to bed. So I stopped, but I had an attitude and after about 10 minutes I went to bed on my own. Mother shouted up the stairs "and you better use the bathroom before you go to bed!" So I did that first then I went to bed.

Monday is here and I've finally started the program! I'm excited all over again and ready to meet my new friends. They picked me up in a van just like the other people did. It was fun; they played music and asked us questions.

When we arrived at the building I was the first one out of my seat belt. They showed us where to go and they had activities ready and set up for us. I was having a good time and then it came close to the end of it. It was almost time for us to go back home. Didn't want to, but then I did. It was home.

My sister Hope answered the door when I got home. And who'd I ask for? Mother. I always did. I asked her where mom was, and she said mother hadn't got home yet. She said mom stopped to get us groceries for dinner and some snacks. Hope said we were having spaghetti and green beans and lemonade.

Here comes mother finally banging at the front door. Hope and I rush to the door to help mother with the bags. We rush in and out of the house until we've gotten them all. Finally we finish and mom goes upstairs to wash up and get ready to make dinner. I'm very hungry and can't wait for dinner to be done already. At the program I go to, they make us eat healthy and sometimes we're allowed a snack.

Dinner was good but its bed time now and I'm tired anyway. Tonight was a rare night. She didn't bother me and when she woke me up to go use the bathroom, she did it without banging my door open and hitting the walls. I was able to go back to sleep and wake up just fine.

As soon as I get home I tell mom about my friends. She gets angry, really angry. She starts saying how dumb I am and looks in Hope's direction to continue saying what she'll do if I don't shut up.

I've always been the outcast. Mother never raised my sisters to treat me the same way they treated each other, nor did she teach them to understand my condition. I am just like them. We are all the same. I may learn slower and my mind may not process information the same as theirs but I am still an aunt, a big sister, little sister, a woman, her daughter, I am human.

I have a heart, and I have feelings too. What a difference it would've been had she loved me more and beat me less. Had she cared more and hated me less. If she had taken the time to help me learn, my temper would not have existed and I never even needed all the medication she put me on. It was only needed if they were already prescribed.

I decided to go for another walk. This one was different because I didn't plan on coming back. Luckily Hope had just arrived from school. I left the front door open and Hope noticed I wasn't home. She ended up looking around to see if someone had broken in.

I thought I had gotten far enough but she saw me at the top of our street. I just stood there and looked at her. She told me to come back so I did. I stopped half way and asked if I was in trouble. She said no and I told her to please not tell mom.

We went back inside and mother got home shortly after. After dinner I went to bed and I tried to dream. I didn't want to be here anymore. One time I tried to cut myself but I couldn't do it. I just couldn't, I was too afraid. Though mother tried hard to convince me I was crazy, I couldn't really do much damage to myself. I wasn't crazy, but living with her made me feel all kinds of ways. That had been the last time I tried running away. I was tired of that. Eventually for a little while it became routine for me to eat and sleep and not speak to anyone.

I had to remind myself that I have sisters and that Hope is my baby sister and I'm her big sister. Hope helped me a lot with my memory. She'd tell me about our family and reassure me. We looked at family photos all the time and we'd go through them all. That helped a lot.

The time had come for another family gathering. All my sisters were bringing my nieces and nephews. Hope helped me remember them too. Hope never liked the fact that I had to take medication. When she saw me take it, I'd ask if I could throw it away. She'd tell me to go ahead.

Family is here! It's time for everyone to be extremely loud for no reason and to eat some grilled food. We'd grill all the time. We'd have hot dogs, hamburgers and chicken. The only bad thing was the alcohol. They'd drink so much and smoke sometimes too. But tonight mom really did a number. She drank a little too much.

I tried asking her about the facility and my friends. She didn't want to hear that at all. So we went back and forth and she decided to hit me. But it doesn't stop there. Now we're on the floor and she's on top of me.

Mother repeatedly pounded my face with her fists. Blackened and swelled up my eye. She wouldn't stop until one of my older sisters took her off of me. The woman was mad, insane. All I could do was look in the mirror and shake my head.

Hope and Allison were crying outside while mother fought me. Hope had the look of fury and she had wondered why no one was trying to stop mother from beating me. The one time I can recall winning any battle with her was the day I bit her. But that's another story.

The night quickly ended soon after that. My sisters had come up stairs to check on me. I was wide awake and hungry. They walked with me to the kitchen and let me eat and kept me away from mom. I tried to apologize for making mother mad at me. She didn't want to hear it.

So I gave up and went up to my room to cry. I cried myself to sleep. Tomorrow was Sunday and I hoped we didn't get up for church. Mother made Hope get up and they left. She made me stay home because of my eye. She didn't want to look like the hypocrite she really was. She always knew how to put on a show.

School has started again for Hope. It's her junior year now. Mother has decided to be a foster mom for awhile. She has two boys living with us. I asked one of them if they wanted to be my boyfriend. He said no. I was upset and left him alone. He told mom and she yelled at me to not speak to him again.

So I didn't. The next night she embarrassed me in front of them. She wouldn't answer me when I talked to her and she hit me with her shoe. The boys laughed at me and Hope was furious. Hope choked one of them and mom told her to stop. Mom said they could laugh if they wanted.

Mom told me to go upstairs and get ready for bed. I went to bed. Those boys stayed away from Hope because she was going to get them if they bothered me or laughed at me again. I didn't say a word to them unless they said hi, and then mom would force me to speak.

I could tell Hope didn't like the way mother treated me. But what could she do? Mother had her mind for the most part. Mom was something else. That woman just couldn't get enough of trying to get me to harm myself.

A few days later I ended up in the bathroom. I was on the floor biting myself and scratching myself. The goal was to do what mom said. She wanted to send me away. She wanted the hospital to strap me up and take me.

She'd tell me I belong in the crazy house with the crazy people. She'd say I look crazy all the time and that I act crazy so I needed to go be with the crazy people. So I started to believe her. Did I belong in the crazy house? Probably not, but my mother says so.

When she wasn't around Hope would tell me that I'm not crazy and that I didn't belong in the crazy house but I had already heard it one too many times. I tried to just be crazy like mom said I was. So I bit myself and beat myself in the head. Mom locked the door and said I wasn't ever going back to the program with my friends and that they didn't like me anyway.

What was I to do? I just couldn't take it anymore. She had me right where she wanted me. She tried calling the police on me and that scared me. But she was afraid too. She had never seen me go crazy. She looked as though I was finally out of control and she couldn't handle it.

Finally I settled down and she let me out. Made me wash up and go to bed.

The next day I tried talking to her and she wanted no conversation with me. So I went upstairs to Hope and I talked to her. I asked her why mother hated me so much. I asked her why didn't mother like me. I hurt inside so bad I began to cry.

Hope was sad and she said she didn't know. She told me that mom just doesn't know how to love me. She said it's not my fault and that mom just doesn't have the patience to understand my condition and that mother hadn't accepted that I was sick as a baby.

Hope and I cried. Hope and I said a prayer together for mom. Then Hope prayed for me. Prayer is what has kept this family together and has always kept us grounded. Our faith in prayer is why we are okay today. It's why I'm alive still that's one thing I know. We had to rap up our prayer before mom heard us. Hope went into the bathroom to finish crying. She came out finally and we hugged then talked some more.

I think mom figured out we were bonding and called Hope downstairs to find the remote to the TV.

ENDING

I AM GROWN and alone as I arrived before, when I was only just a development in the womb... Hope is getting closer to graduating. It's coming up on her senior year. Mom told me she's sending me away. I guess that's goodbye. She'd probably been planning this for some time now. She's probably been looking at places she would send me.

The other day she was telling Hope that not many places wanted me. She's trying to put me in places that treat crazy people. I don't want to go. Of course mom is more than happy to be getting rid of me. I want to live with her. I want to stay at home with my mother. She doesn't want me and never has.

I love her any how. No one understands, but it's deeply unconditional. I'm only confused about how she feels about me. I always try to stay out of trouble and do what she says. I try to be good so she'll at least like me. Not much luck has come my way though. Maybe going away won't be so bad.

I'll miss home and I'll miss mother. I love my sisters very much. They could come around more often and maybe take me out sometimes. But it's always a fun time whenever they do visit. I haven't seen them in awhile. Everyone works and the kids are in school. I've been home alone lately. Mom goes and comes back as soon as she can.

Hope is home from school and she's outside in a truck. I think it's her teacher. She comes inside and I hug her. She asked me where was mom. So I told her mom left for a little while and that I was home by myself. She looked frustrated after I told her that. She asked me where did mom go and was I alright. I was fine; I napped most of the day.

I ate before mom left and that was awhile ago. I'm pretty hungry now so Hope and I made a snack. Peanut butter and jelly sandwiches never failed us. The door knob turns and its mom with a few grocery bags. She made Hope come into the living room to talk to her about me leaving.

She found a place. Hope told her that her teacher was telling her before he dropped her off that if she sent me away he'd have nothing to do with her anymore. He said to Hope that mother was supposed to take of me and that I'm her child no matter what. I wish mom felt the same. He completely disagreed with mom sending me away.

Mother had her mind made up. She was happy she finally found a place for me. It was just going to be a process that took a few months. Hope didn't like it. Mother told her it was a good place and that I'd be ok.

I could tell Hope was sad. Mom also tried explaining that she didn't mean to leave me home alone. Said she had to handle business. Hope just looked as if she were picturing bad things while mother spoke to her. Hope was pretty upset with mom.

It was almost dinner time and Hope and I were waiting for mom to get started. Hope didn't know what to do. She had no control over the situation. She was always defending me and tried to lookout for me as often as possible. Such a shame having to be protective over me even though I'm an adult. It must have been difficult for her.

She does well in school and mom is proud of her. Every now and again she'll still try to go over alphabets with me or color, even do puzzles with me. Mrs. Gwen would buy me puzzles all the time. Mrs. Gwen kept puzzles at her house. I've been missing her too.

During dinner I asked about Mrs. Gwen. Mother said she'd call Mrs. Gwen so I could speak to her. Mrs. Gwen was getting really old. I love her very much. She's been in my life ever since birth. That lady has been apart of our family forever. She's always helping mother with whatever she needs.

It's a bright early Monday morning. Mom wakes me up to go run errands with her so I wouldn't be left alone. She had told Hope that she was getting a caretaker to sit with me at home until she got home. I was happy to hear that. No more being home alone.

The caretaker came over to meet me and talk to me for awhile with mother. They talked about her working hours and when to give me my medicine. The lady seemed nice. She said she would take me out sometimes. She realized I was at home too much and never really got out much.

Hope took me to the park sometimes but she didn't like going out much. When we did go it was fun. We'd talk sometimes about flowers and animals and food. She'd talk about anything I wanted to talk about.

After awhile I got lazy and didn't really want to go out much. I think I'm going to like my caretaker though. She is nice and likes to eat like me. She's kind of big and has chubby cheeks. Her name is Ms. Ashley. She starts tomorrow and she's going to bring me cookies. I can't wait for her to come back with those.

Ms. Ashley is leaving and mom wants to talk to me. Not so polite though. She yelled at me to behave and not cause trouble. She said I'd have to deal with her if I gave the lady any trouble. I told her I would be good. I told her not to worry.

Night came too soon. It was time to get ready for bed. I was ready to spend time with Ms. Ashley. Especially enjoying those cookies, I hope they're chocolate chip cookies.

I'm up before mom this time. She came to wake me up but I was already using the bathroom. I had begun to brush my teeth and she bust open the bathroom door. Smack! Right into me. Why? I knew it was intentional but what could I do. So she yelled at me to hurry up and get dressed so I can eat breakfast and be ready for Ashley.

She was only staying with me until Hope got home from school. That was nice of her. I started to get a bit impatient. As soon as I was getting ready to ask mom when Ashley was coming, she came to the door. Mother let her in and the first thing I noticed were the cookies. She was happy to see me and I was happy to eat those cookies. And they were chocolate chip!

First day with Ms. Ashley was good. We talked a lot and watched TV. Mom came home early and stayed in her room. I was glad she did. She left us alone and let the lady do her job.

Hope finally arrived and I was excited to tell her about Ashley. Hope was happy to see me happy. Ashley greeted Hope, and then she had to leave. She said goodbye to us all and said she'd see me tomorrow. Mom told me to keep being good and that I wouldn't be here much longer.

I got upset with her. She knows I don't want to go away. I told her I didn't care. She charged at me and struck me repeatedly against my head and neck and my back. I told her to stop and that she was hurting me. She yelled for me to shut up.

She told me that I was going to be gone and for me to get over it. Mother said she was sick of me and that no one wanted to take care of me or watch over me. So for awhile I never spoke of it again. Again she had hurt my feelings. Hope went upstairs to cry. I knocked on her door and she let me in to give her a hug. I went into my room after checking on her.

Mother came upstairs and heard Hope crying. She threatened Hope that if she kept crying she would get a whooping. So Hope begged her not to and she stopped crying. Hope went into the bathroom to clean up and then we got ready for dinner.

Ashley is back and I have a temper. I'm not in the mood to converse or anything. She bought cupcakes today and I didn't want those either. She asked me what was wrong. I told her nothing. Then she started staring at me. I didn't like that at all.

So I told her to stop staring at me. I began to shout at her and yell at her to leave me alone. She saw my neck and asked me what happened. So I just said it out of frustration. I told her mom hit me. She was shocked and found it hard to believe. She asked why and I told her mom is mad at me.

She said she was going to call someone. Later that day when she was getting ready to leave, I realized she called someone from social services. Mother was furious and told the lady the only lie she was good at. She tried telling her I had an episode and that I started hitting and scratching myself.

The lady took that as bullshit and said that I was a sweet smart girl. She left and she quit and said she would pray for us. Mother didn't think I told her anything. My older sister Olivia had met her and spoke with her also. For some reason mom was more suspicious with her.

Mother had to find someone else now. She was also questioned by social services. Eventually this situation boiled down and was left alone. A few weeks later she spoke with Mrs. Gwen. It had been awhile. I talked to Mrs. Gwen and asked her when she was going to come visit me.

Mrs. Gwen came to visit me a couple days later. She left me money and brought over some groceries. She said she would try to come over again soon. Mrs. Gwen was really old now. Her husband had to drive. They are both very old. Ms. Gwen stayed as long as she could and talked to me awhile.

I didn't want her to go. She said she'd call me more to check on me. I missed her so much. She would keep me a lot as a child. My twin and I. She asked about Penelope too. Penelope was very distant and had my niece to take care of. I haven't seen Penelope in a very long time.

The months have finally flown by. Mother didn't find another caretaker. But the facility I'll be living at had called mother earlier. When she got home from work she heard their message and started thanking God.

I knocked on her door and asked her what the people said. She told me that I was finally leaving and getting out of the house. I told her I wanted to stay with her and she didn't want to hear it. I started to get emotional and I ran to Hope. Hope held me and I cried.

Hope was angry with mother and didn't want to be near her at this time. After that Hope let me stay in her room and watch TV then I left to go in my own room and lay down. I no longer wanted to be bothered. Mom told Hope the news and that they'd be coming to get me in a few days.

Those few days were flying by. I so badly wanted to stay home with mother. She helped me pack up everything I needed. I had to be ready early. They were coming in the morning while Hope would be in school. So the night before I left Hope hugged me tight and told me she loves me and that she'll call and check on me. She told me to be good and have fun. I told her I'll miss her and that she should come visit me.

The next morning I left and mom walked me to the van. She didn't hug me but she waved goodbye. I watched her close the front door as I was leaving. I cried myself to sleep.

A Mother's Love

Day and night I yearn for you
Like a flower without water
And whatever life is left in me
Whithers away like dead leaves

Noon and dawn I cry and cry
For your sweet embrace my heart aches
There is no one to take your place
Who holds your smile and beautiful face

Deeply and dearly I love you so
It is A Mother's Love I've yet to know

Printed in the United States
By Bookmasters